what remains

Poems by Dawne Leiker

Spartan
Press

Spartan Press

Kansas City, Missouri

spartanpresskc.com

Spartan
Press

Acknowledgments:

Special thanks to my sister, Janet Carman, for her relentless
support of whatever project I dream up.

Also, special thanks to the editors of these publications where
some of these poems were first published in some form or
another:

"Deer Crossing" was published in *Moving Force Journal,*
"Late Show" was published in *Coffin Bell,*
"Reasons," "Cave Paintings," and "*Riddle*" were featured on
    an online zine *150kansaspoems*.wordpress.com
"Red Rover" and "Cave Paintings" were published in the
    Broadkill Review

TABLE OF CONTENTS

It is just an illusion we have here on Earth that one moment follows another one, like beads on a string, and that once a moment is gone it is gone forever.

– Kurt Vonnegut, *Slaughterhouse-Five*

To the memory of my loving, creative, and ever-encouraging parents.

Reasons

Without fail, each August, I stop to wonder
why my great grandparents stayed
where ruts crack beneath the
crisps of weeds
and only bindweed dares to thrive.
Tough, stern-faced, they battled the earth
to coax seeds into grains,
while black "Dust Bowl" blizzards choked
hot curses from their mouths.

They must have had their reasons.
Maybe the charlatans, strange ways,
or ill fit of the world outside
corralled them back to the familiar.
Where roots and worms tangle
in living earth.
Where locusts raise metallic songs
to a cloudless ocean of sky.
Where sunset's red glow
exhales their timeless breath.

Today the August breeze cools my skin.
The sun is not a searing enemy.
I search the ground for cracks and find
velvety grass and globs of spongy earth.
I kneel on the green space where I see
ground uncracked and breathing a promise.

I imagine their fallen bones,
buried in the Lone Star graveyard,
my ancestors' dust blended with ancient dirt.
Would they feel my hands
digging in fragrant soil?
Feel the weight of me
tethered where they settled?

For one brief summer, drought
is a word not spoken.
This land seems friendly.
A place to be touched.
But I know well enough,
ditches shining with puddles will not last.

Soon after barren clouds tease the horizon
I'll see cracks checker through
the drying weeds, where sky meets earth
on a straight-ruled line.

Today, though. Today, I press mud, fat
against the roots of basil and mint.
Touch the promise of
impatiens' purple blooms.
Listen for the distant thunder.
Listen, like my forbearers, for the rustle
of crops on the vast rippling plains.
Cling to the hope of rain-bearing clouds.
Unpack the reasons to leave.
Bury them deep beneath the busted sod.

Finding Pa

The story goes, it was dusk when Ma Jones and the kids arrived at
Orlando's homestead after a rough journey in a canvas-covered
    wagon.

He hadn't thought to write them. Tell them where he was headed.
But Ma figured she'd try the Kansas address where his Civil War
    pension checks had been sent.

Wapello County's raw wind had ripped through his chest since
    the war.
Aggravated the ailments that followed his chronic dysentery
since his discharge from the 22nd Iowa Infantry, just after
    Vicksburg fell.
Nights in shallow trenches shared with mud-encrusted farm boys.
Days of living and dying among vermin under bloody sunsets.

I picture Ma, eyes blazing, sitting atop a hand-stitched quilt
on the wagon's seat. She's worn, sunburned, firm jawed.

Then I see Lenora, brown braids, yellow gingham, walking
    alongside the wagon.
A toothy grin, like Laura Engels Wilder, searching the horizon
    for traces of Pa.

She sees white primrose in the tall grass bending away from
   the sherbet sun,
Pa cleaning his dugout barn, as the wagon clatters up then stops.

He's just taken a pitchfork full of manure to the door to throw
   on the pile
when he hears old Charley's familiar neigh.

But he stands there, pitchfork mid-air, staring in silence at his
   family
'til he gets ahold of himself, throws the shit on a pile, then says,
   "Hello".

what remains

She stopped to listen to the prairie wind
shushing through the wheatgrass. Shushing the wails
of long dead women and children,
settled within the bluffs.

Battleground. Massacre ground. Holy ground.
Countless times, Lenora had walked the crooked path
along middle Sappa Creek,
brushy black with beaver dams.

She bent low to the dirt, uncovering
a few shiny shells. Closed her eyes, imagining
the girl who had worn them. The shells, strung together
on a leather band, fastened with a tiny knot
upon a graceful neck of one
perhaps no older than she.

Earth have pity.
Sky, see your daughters.
It is a good day to die.

Three years before Lenora's family had arrived in Kansas,
an eerie morning fog had obscured the middle Sappa.

Blue coat soldiers and buffalo hunters
trapped native people like jack rabbits.
Targeted for extermination. Their bodies
burned within their lodges. Empty cartridge cases
piled high along the surrounding ridge.

Late afternoon shadows fell, and Lenora placed
the shells in her flour sack, with beads
newly dug from the dirt and ash, and
turned back to her timber claim.

Inside her apron pocket, she touched S.R.'s letter.
Mouthed the words to his poem:
Thy love mayest look both long and loud
For one more true, bold, brave, and proud
But love serene is the golden shroud
To which prince and peasant oft have bowed.

She'd answered his letters as he crossed
Nebraska, Wyoming, Idaho, to Oregon.
Told him of her claim at the foot of a hill.
The lonely nights. The kiss upon her lips
readied for his return.
The child within her grew heavy.
The air above her, heavier still.

Her morning glories now grow thick
along the wooden fence, as she shares with visitors
her last cupful of Indian beads and relics.
The Sappa Creek massacre spoken of
from time to time. Her son, tousled hair,
rises, sleepy-eyed from his lumpy mattress.
S.R., just up the draw, pitches hay into the wagon.

It's the foggy days, that give Lenora pause.
Days when there's nothing left to do but imagine.
Squinting, she looks toward Sappa Creek.
Are blue coats hidden in the gray shroud of dawn?
Is smoke rising from blazing lodges?
She closes her eyes, but knows
the burnt offerings of those who came before
are borne across the prairie morn.
Laid silently upon the claim now settled.

Dream Trading

Homestead.
Home place.
Home.
She told him that's what he wanted.
That her days were dark and desperate without him.
He held out as long as he could.
'Til that day he washed his hands of the charlatans,
their dubious offers of gain.
'Til that day he sold his last three good saddle horses,
at Grand Junction, "tolerable cheap."
All that remained of the wild ones he'd run in
across Oregon, Idaho, Nevada, Utah.
Lonesome country.
Snow so bad over the Rockies,
he couldn't cross on horseback.
He caught the train at Gunnison. Bound for Kansas.
Married her weeks later.
His days of "disagreeable camping out," behind him.
He'd come home.

The Pioneer and Dad

January babes, both.
Sam crossed the U.S. to see the Wild West.
Dad crossed an ocean to fight the Good War.
I pour a glass of red and search for songs to celebrate my Y-DNA.

First, the pioneer, great grandpa Sam. His song: "Days of '49".
The song folks say Sam recited the afternoon he died. He wasn't
a singer, it is said, but he could sure as hell recite the words.
For Sam, "Days of '49" must have captured the hope, the
heartbreak, and the dreams he found on the trails west.

Of the comrades all that I've had, there's none that's left to boast
And I'm left alone in my misery like some ol' poor wandering
ghost

There is no frontier brutishness in tattered photos of Sam. I
imagine that he moved with grace, almost elegantly. Like my dad.
It's hard work to carry oneself with such ease.

I give thanks for Sam, the pioneer, cowboy, horse trader,
railroader, trapper, who stayed in Kansas to raise his family. Who
settled. Therefore, I am.

Now for Dad, who might have been an engineer, were it not for a plane crash and a world war. He settled in a small Kansas town because home was a rare gift to savor, after soldiering through Alaska, Australia, New Guinea, and the Philippines.

I fill my glass again and begin his song: "Stardust". Dad liked the way the melody lingered just so, falling unexpectedly and then lifting effortlessly. That's what he liked. For everything to feel effortless. Like the silken voice of Nat King Cole, meandering the flawless refrain:

You wander down the lane and far away
Leaving me a song that will not die
Love is now the stardust of yesterday

Sometimes I see Dad in my dreams, and he asks me when I'll
    come home.

Maybe I'll do that when I finish
Sipping
Singing
Dreaming
Waking
Holding ghosts of the pioneer and dad within my skin.

Home with Skylights, Pets Allowed

Out of the pitch of a July night, laughter, beers,
broken windows.
Rowdies mopped the kitchen floor
with the scarecrow head of the loudest one.
Never again the smell of warm chocolate cake
cooling on the embroidered tablecloth.
Nor steam rising from the cast iron tub
as they scrubbed their skin pink.
Just the sputter of a rusted Chrysler down the crunchy lane.
And the pedal grinder scraping against the pickup bed.
Then cattle came to flatten the wild lilacs.
Hoofprints and mounds of dung encircled the foundation
And one found his way in.
And another.
Then a coyote, rats, doves and hornets.
A zoo of wild and domestic animals right here
Where she painted flowers on the wall
Where he lay in bed day after day after the war
Where kids splashed in the pond
just beyond the folk's view.
Now there's just the screech of the rusty windmill
and slits of sunlight through the failing roof.

But the gray, lifeless house waits for human eyes
to weep for the family's toil that crumbled in the sun,
beneath the herds who fed here.
Beneath the trampled, unremembered dreams.

Hush

Long years past, daughter of the pioneers
lifted her window to breathe ripened cherries,
a hymn of praise on her lips.
She looped and knotted doilies and white lace.
Arranged triangles of carrot and raisin sandwiches.

Ever she mourned with the milky sky
the crumbled sod house of her birth,
the plainness of the prairie covering her loved ones.

Cradled, then bent by Kansas winds
I knew her only at the dimming of her days.
Silver hair loosened from its tightly wound knot.

Her whispers heard only in the hush of white linens.

Ivory Ghosts

Beethoven rages
from the shadow of the stairway.
Mutters his disgust.
Fumbling fingers tempted him
to hover above his weathered obelisk,
shoot instantly across the ocean.
Cover his deaf ears
as Sonata Pathetique is stabbed mercilessly
in my living room.

I bite my bottom lip,
race mechanically to the last bar,
Strain to use proper fingering.
Sigh.
Silence.

Beethoven's passionate eyes
fade into wallpaper.
I stash the sonata
between volumes of Mozart and Bach.

Within the hinged piano bench, worn pages.
Dreamy eyed, a tousled brunette kisses the man on the moon.
"Dear Old Dixie Moon."

Gently, the faded notes come to life,
Chords roll, words touch my lips.
So tell her with your beams she's ever in my dreams...

The keys remember her.
How she felt her way along each one 'til the song was complete.
Sang aloud when no one was listening.
Dreamed she could kiss the moon.

I heard the sad business of her dying too young.
Saw her gentle features only in photo albums.
I thumb through the frayed pages of her music.
Touch her piano's keys and sing her spirit.

Packed away, Beethoven grumbles from his grave,
while Ellen lets me play.

The Last Red Glow

Through pastures, dusty roads, weedy ditches,
he scanned the ground for remnants of ancient life.
Lifted tiny measures of solid earth.
Fragments altered by tools or machines. Others still
    untouched.
Against a blue horizon, he traced their outline,
then dropped the rocks into his front pocket.

From the corner of his bed, after dark,
He struck a piece of flint with hammer stone.
Chipping arrowheads to Carson's monologue.
Then, drawing the last red glow from his Camel,
stashed the rocks in a coffee can.
Slid the can under his wooden bed frame.

A quarter of the rocks are mine.
Stored in a plastic box with red lid.
A ripped piece of a cardboard label
identifies the rare artifacts
in Dad's handwriting:
Bob Bannister
9-2-79
4-1-82

Gray and buff sandstone, quartzite, igneous.
All smell like plastic, not earth, not Old Spice.
After 30 years secured in Rubbermaid
miles away from Bob Bannister's pasture.
Decades removed from Dad's storm-beat hands.

It was his left hand that smashed the lead glass
when a stroke ended his last summer day.
Shards of glass from the bookshelf near the bed
fell on gold carpet branded by cigarette burns.
In a pasture, hot wind scattered dust from hidden rocks.

Did he see past the horizon, the rain-bearing clouds?
Did he kick at buffalo grass with the toe of his boots,
revealing hidden treasures? Ancient artifacts?
His pulse raced and there was no trace of him
left in his eyes. No answer on his lips.

Enfolding his fingers, I touched a measure of ancient lives.
Golden images passing on a distant road.
The life-giving ancestors illumining his way.
I traced their outline against antiseptic walls
and saw the red glow of sunset inhale his breath,
as living earth embraced her dying son.

Top Shelf Whiskey

Could just as well be water
in that quart Mason jar
Rusty metal ring, dusty lid.
But the fiery magic of moonshine
waits silently,
reflecting sunlight through the west window.
Seems it could have been forgotten
Twenty years past Prohibition
No one had sipped a drop.

But weathered hands
lift the jar from its spot on the top shelf
of the wooden shed.
Unscrew the lid
with quiet reverence.
Pour a spoonful
as wide-eyed young one waits.

The old man pulls a match
from the pocket of his bib overalls,
strikes it on the wooden shelf.
Neither breathes as he touches
the spark to the moonshine.

The blue flame arcs above the spoon
Red heart at the center,
golden tongue at the crown.
Spellbound, both are mute
until the flame burns out.

Oooo, do it again.
Maybe later, says the old man.
Did you ever drink any?
Never, no, never.   Like as not it'd kill me.
Smells like the doctor's office.
Yep.

The old man had ground the corn,
more than twenty years back.
Soaked it in hot water in the still.
Dumped in yeast so the mash would ferment.
Portioned it out in his ma's canning jars.

Folks said blue flames meant the shine was safe
but red flames... Well, they said,
"Lead burns red and makes you dead."

From the rumpled blankets
down the hall from Grandad's rattling snores

the young one dreams of blue flame

dancing on a silver spoon.

Dreams one day he'll hold the magic Mason jar.

Unscrew the lid and ignite the white lightening

as youngsters murmur   Oooo

Marveling at the alchemy

of antique moonshine.

Cave Paintings

She painted the monkey on the wall
years before I was born. But there's
something in its eyes that makes me
think of me. The way it glances
up and to the right. The way I do
when I don't know the answer,
but don't want to say.

Only rarely over the years
did we drive the weeded lane
to the gray stucco home place,
empty since my birth and Dad's town job.
We'd survey the outbuildings' decay,
bending to collect rusted implements
from the patches of dirt and buffalo grass,
gathering fragrant lilacs and pink rhubarb stalks
from the overgrown garden.

One summer night, we lingered at the farm
past sunset. My brother lifted
a torn mattress from the back porch
and pushed it onto the brown dirt.

We flopped down on our backs,
wishing for tiny white stars
to sail across the blanket of night.
I closed my eyes just for an instant,
weary from breathing country air.
"See the shooting star?"
he asked, pointing into the darkness,
to where I had just missed it.

Missed, too, the farm that wasn't my home.
Vacant now more than five decades,
but for two dead coyotes in its basement,
an assortment of snakes, birds, and rats.
And Mom's crude murals on the walls. Curious,
fading traces of her dream to be an artist.
To be a mother. To be a decorator,
without money to do it tidy.

Down the dank, ancient stairway, cowboys
cling to the block foundation.
One is masked, a Lone Ranger, pink pistol
on his hip. He rides a curly yellow horse.
Across the room, another cowboy
shoots a pistol into the air,
thrusting high its crooked barrel.

Upstairs, red cuckoo clock on the kitchen wall,
framed by a mosaic of cracked ivory paint,
forever strikes seven. Beneath it,
a metal oven, filled with debris,
is now cold to the touch.

Teddy bear and wolf murals
tend the children's room.
The little ones would have been tucked in
by seven. My brother's spanking finished moments ago.
My sister's brown curls laid across
a feather pillow.

And me, alien to the memories
stored here. I touch the paw of
the monkey on the wall, who
fixes his eyes up and to the right.
He does not know. He cannot say
If the light that shot across the night
Was ever really there.

Rock Opera

Five, maybe six, people know why the rock matters.
A quarter moon-shaped blonde chunk of limestone.
It lays now on a bed of river rock. A garden gnome
naps nearby, unimpressed that the limestone
stood solid as trains clattered through Hays City
in the wild 1870s. That it held firm against lightening,
against gunshots, against scorching dry summers.
Hauled by horse and wagon from a quarry south of town,
the limestone chunk joined other native stones
in an impressive three-story structure.
Locally mixed mortar somehow held
the Opera House together for more than a century.
The rock had no eyes to see, but he warmed
to the presence of women in lace-wrapped gowns,
men in smart black top hats gathering within his walls.
He swelled with pride as painted scenery backdrops
rolled across his stage.
When the mortar turned to dust, fellow stones
fell to the sidewalk outside the silent building.
Handbills tacked to the cracked doors read, "Keep out.
Premises condemned by the City of Hays."
A wrecking ball labored only a few hours to scatter
mammoth heaps of limestone across the corner lot.

Pigeons, rats, mice deserted, searching out a new home.
The rock, though, had no home. It lay atop fellow stones
who had stood with it against the wicked Kansas winds
for more than a century. The trains still rumbled by,
but no stones trembled with anticipation of a fine visitor.
No opera the Sunday morning I climbed
the orange construction fence, searched the rubble,
lifted the perfect quarter-moon blonde chunk of stone
and carried it to my trunk.
A tiny rim of light kisses the limestone's scalloped edge.
From the rock garden, the stone and I watch the moon lift
above our neighbor's roof. A light breeze ruffles me
but not the rock.
The rock knows he will outlive me, just as he survived long after
the men who fashioned him into an opera house.
Just as he survived centuries beyond the fishes of the deep
who gave him small regard when he was sediment
in an ancient sea. For this solitary evening, he is king
of the rock garden. A jewel among the gnomes.

The Request

That summer of stale carnations, saccharine lilies, musky mums,

I stopped short every time the phone rang.

Farm accident.

Heart attack.

Car wreck.

Random deaths. But in a small town   Unsettling.

Behind velveteen curtains, cold bodies in bronze caskets.

I raised a tinny vibrato on the mortuary organ

Face hidden by dog-eared sheet music.

The Rose

Left hand, pounding a monotony of quarter notes

Right hand, dutifully slogging the pedantic melody.

(I say love; it is a flower)

Sobs from the front row

For the empty crib.

I willed a wall of black notes

Between my heart and the mother's tears

Choked the smog of funeral flowers.

Under the music, cloudy faces of family members,

Grandma, Cousin Boomer, Dad,

All once displayed here.

Tongues of candle shadows had mocked their stillness
Plastic non-expressions imprinted. Packaged for eternity
(Far beneath the bitter snow)
Wrapped in the wails of young motherhood,
Blue light filtered through the stained glass window.
Measure by measure, hanging on 'til the final bar line.
I drew strains of life from notes on old sheet music
For a twenty-dollar bill
Tucked in a plain white envelope.

The Seige

It was a hot and drowsy Saturday afternoon, when I first
    wondered about Mother.

"Read me a story?" I took a bite out of my butter and sugar
    sandwich and sat on the floor, cross-legged in front of her.

"What sort of story?" Mother asked. She was lying on the sofa,
    propped up on one elbow.

"That one. The one you were reading just now."

She picked up the magazine. The cover showed two women
    bending over a dead horse, appearing to cut off chunks of its
breast meat. Fur-covered remains lay atop a sled in the
    foreground of the picture. Mother flipped through the pages,
then lowered the magazine. Looked into my eyes.

"Did I ever tell you about the Siege of Leningrad?"

"No,"

"Here's your World War II history lesson for today, dear."

I was seven years old and didn't know much about war. What I
    did know was that my dad had been to a war and that he
didn't talk about it. That his olive-green wool uniform was
    stored in our attic. It smelled like mothballs and had ribbons
and patches on its shoulders.

"During World War II, people in Leningrad… Russia. Sorry,
    Russia, if you didn't know… were cut off from all food and
supplies by German soldiers. Two million people starved to
    death. It lasted 872 days." She pointed to the magazine cover.

"Horse meat," she said. "Those folks were lucky to find it."

My eyes widened. I swallowed hard, the butter and sugar wadding
    up in my throat.

"There's a poem here. About the siege. About…. Well, just let me
    read it." She read, in a faraway sing-song voice:

And for supper, clearly,
I'll need a little baby.
I'll take the neighbor's,
Steal him from his cradle.

I tried to look away, so she wouldn't see the redness around
my eyes. But she saw my panic, and that delighted her.

"Did you know that I moved to Kansas from Russia?" she
said, with a grin.

"No."

"Did you know that once you taste a child, nothing ever tastes
as sweet?" She licked her lips. then after a long silence,
laughed, dropping the magazine to the floor.

Alien at the Farm

When you brought me home to meet them, your family was
wary of me, a town girl in platform sandals, stumbling through
the dirt clods. You were my first real boyfriend, and I hoped
they'd like me. But your dad shook his head and laughed when
I asked the cows' names, sniggered when I waved "hello" to the
horses grazing near the red picture-book barn. Your mom eyed
me at the dinner table, as I pushed pork fat around my plate with
a knife.

This is how an alien would feel, I thought, visiting earth for
the first time. Beamed inside a farmhouse deep in a southwest
Nebraska canyon. Repulsed by a wad of pork fat.

I'd met your older brother Buddy a couple of times at the pool
hall. I had never seen him sober. A six-pack under his pickup
seat, he kept an empty for spitting his Skoal juice. As I recall, he
was supposed to be in charge of most livestock operations at the
farm.

It was Buddy's turn to watch the hogs, one frosty October night.
The night they were farrowing/miscarrying.

The night the pig fetuses needed him most.

We arrived the next morning, as Buddy snored on the sofa.
In the farrowing house, baby hogs, like molded gray gelatin,
littered the hard mud. Tiny snouts and hooves peeking from
cold mounds of blood.

You used a spatula to scrape them from the mud, scoop
them into brown paper bags to bury in the north pasture.
It was pointless to cry, you told me. The piglets didn't really
have a chance.

You smelled of blood and pig shit when we shared a
morning Budweiser in your dad's Chevy truck. You said not
to tell that Buddy was drunk again or about the gelatinous
pigs.

Don't worry, you said, when we get married, we'll live in
town.

The Goodbye Girls

Never lifting their white faces to the road
The girls disregarded your pickup's sputtering start.
Ambled through Texas sandburs
to the salt lick.

The day you left the home place,
Annabelle strained her neck through the fence line,
trying to get at the good grass near the trailer.
Dixie laid in the sun flicking flies away,
with her expert tail.

The nubby tan grass, half eaten by critters,
Smelled of promissory notes and repossession.
Auctioneer's cadence borne on a watercolor sky.
Sleight of hand – a number swept the air
Then the act was finished.

You tossed your work boots in a cardboard box.
Dropped into a rolling chair under cheap fluorescent lights.
Checked the forecast
for talk of rain.
Polaroid of the old girls in your shirt pocket.

Riddle

She answers the riddles no one can
The punchlines to jokes we didn't know we started.
We mull her words, wonder where they were born.
She says the five of us sat on the davenport
'til the wind blew us away. She laughs,
picturing of the nonsense of it.
Her head slumped low, she doesn't see
that five of us sit there. Just listening.
She asks why God doesn't fall from the sky
And if pioneers ate grass when they ran out of food.
She asks the name of the little boy in the red sweater
Who no one else can see.
Who loves her scraping, high-pitched songs
that stab our ears and twist our hearts.
She answers the riddles no one can
From the corner of the room
when no one knows she's listening.

The Art of Conversation

"What do you suppose Dad's doing?"
I glance at her drooping eyes.
"I know he's dead," she continues,
But what do you suppose he's doing?"
"Sitting on a cloud?" I venture.
"Golfing with an angel?"
She giggles, wrinkling her nose.
"Someday we will all be together,
And we will be so happy," she says,
fidgeting with a thread I can't see.
Her blue-veined fingers tremble.
"But you have to get out of here now."
"I will. But. Later," I say.
Then, for long moments, she is silent.
I touch her gray hair, soft as feathers.
Down the hallway, alarms beg nurses
For the privilege of toileting,
For the comfort of a blanket,
For the blessing of a smile.
"I'm not sure how I'll get out of here,"
Her voice, now shrill.

"They might have to shoot me."

She shuts her eyes, touching a finger to her lips.

"I think Dad moved Mom's body,

She was buried one place,

But now she's not."

Confined

Through gold orange campfire flames
She saw teepees surrounding
The black night at the house on First Street
And she shut her eyes
And the flames twisted into faceless dancers
And she covered her ears
And still heard the rhythm of rawhide drums
Next morning, startled her sister
When she told what she saw
How many pills had she taken?
Blue ones? White ones?
To stop the visions she didn't sleep
But blazing eyes watched her
Blue ones. White ones. How many.
Wheeled down the narrow hallway
Past black doorways to private hells
From the corner of her dank room
A tall man watched her
I called her from a shadow in my basement
Whispered how are you? and held my breath
She said her feet were blue

A horrible long hair had grown from her chin

How are you? she asked.

I'm fine. Everyone's fine.

This place is bitter as winter, she said

The people gray and icy

Could I come soon - take her back to the hills?

So she could see sage brush dotting the sunlit valleys

Warm her feet by the crackling orange flames?

Daughter of the Moon

Big-Sea-Water. I puzzled to think how it must have shone. The black and gloomy pine trees rising in the forest behind it. I looked out across a horizon of tan prairie sliced by robin's egg blue sky and wondered at the world of Nokomis, daughter of the Moon, Nokomis.

The rhythm of "Song of Hiawatha" is a part of me. On-hold music from my mom, who memorized Henry Wadsworth Longfellow's 1855 epic poem at the Lawn Ridge Country School in northwest Kansas. Her voice teased out its rhymes, sing-songing the words over and over.

I imagine her schoolmates standing close to a pot belly stove, holding their readers, repeating the rhythmic words:

By the shores of Gitche Gumee,
By the shining Big-Sea-Water,
Stood the wigwam of Nokomis.
Daughter of the Moon, Nokomis.

Mom had a way of twisting the poem, using the words to fill in the gaps of an endlessly uneventful Kansas day. She'd recite its stanzas, starting at chapter three, "Unremembered Ages", then smile a slightly wicked smile, delighting at my shocked face when she got to the part where the "wrinkled old Nokomis nursed the little Hiawatha."

That irritated me. I liked to imagine I was
Hiawatha, rocked in a linden cradle:
Bedded soft in moss and rushes,

Safely bound with reindeer sinews.

That like Nokomis, my mother showed me the:
Broad white road in heaven,
Pathway of the ghosts, the shadows,
Running straight across the heavens,
Crowded with the ghosts, the shadows.

But sometimes I couldn't get past the thought of
being nursed by the wrinkled Nokomis.

As close as she could, Mom immersed herself
in American Indian culture. Sioux medicine man Lame
Deer said: "Artists are the Indians of the white world."
She treasured those words, painting portraits, alive with
vibrant colors, of Chief Joseph and Roman Nose…Teepees
surrounding golden tongues of warm campfires.

Afternoon outings sometimes ended with us
getting lost on a winding country road, often in the Arikaree
Breaks. Mom was at home where sagebrush poked my
knobby knees and arrowheads lay beneath a dusty layer of
earth. But it worried me that I couldn't see a paved road
from where we wandered. She would laugh and tell me again
the story of how one morning she'd set out alone to paint a
landscape of that very pasture. Absorbed in her work, she

didn't hear the vagrant approach until he cleared his throat and asked for a ride. She had looked up at him, opened her mouth to say "no." But he backed away, heading for the road, before she could speak. She didn't know why until she glanced in her car's mirror as she backed out the lane. Earlier that morning she had opened paint tubes with her teeth. Black paint had smeared onto her teeth and lips, giving her the face of a late show creature. It delighted her to think she scared that man more than he scared her.

One February afternoon, while naked trees cast shadows outside the nursing home's window, I sat next to Mom's wheelchair, my fingers interlaced with hers.

"Do you still remember Hiawatha's song?" I asked. "By the shores of Gitche Gumme?" Her eyes opened slightly to fix on mine, and she nodded. Then I saw the hint of the wicked smile.

On a good day, she could recite several lines of the poem. But she was weary of a world of too many words. It's sufficient that we shared in our hearts, the words Nokomis taught Hiawatha… Of a rainbow hidden just behind a winter shadow.

'Tis the heaven of flowers you see there;
All the wildflowers of the forest,
All the lilies of the prairie,
When on earth they fade and perish,
Blossom in that heaven above us."

Deer Crossing

Do you see them? I asked my brother. Yes, he said,
barely awake. Two deer, like a mirage, caught in my
      headlights.

They slipped back into darkness after a blink.
Eyes, curious, just like in her painting.
The one that's hung over my piano for years.

I remember she had trouble with their faces.
Yellow paint smeared above her brow, she hunched
over the canvas absorbed in the struggle to make them real.
Laboring to show their gentle spirit as they crossed
the Republican River, framed by the glow of fall foliage.

Now she was nearly gone. Nearly midnight and nearly gone.
At her bedside, I told her I had seen deer outside the
      nursing home.
They posed for us, just like in her painting.

Her eyes, curious, so close to gone, but she knew what I said.
Then a labored breath caught in time, wedged deep in her
      tired lungs.

It seemed the last one she would breathe.

Such a thin, thin thread of life, nearly imperceptible.

One more breath and, yes, now there would be no other.

Confined an eon in the sterile home,

Could she now inhabit painted worlds?

Following spirit guides where gold and crimson leaves

shimmer in the autumn wind. Where winter is no more.

Imp

We stand upon the brink of a precipice. We peer into the abyss—we grow sick and dizzy. Our first impulse is to shrink away from the danger. Unaccountably we remain... it is but a thought, although a fearful one, and one which chills the very marrow of our bones with the fierceness of the delight of its horror. It is merely the idea of what would be our sensations during the sweeping precipitancy of a fall from such a height... for this very cause do we now the most vividly desire it

– Edgar Alan Poe

In the faded photo, my brother smiles
a worried smile. Dirt-caked feet
betraying his ever shoelessness.
While I, sleepy-eyed, bewildered,
stare into the camera. Unaware
of the Imp of the Perverse hovering behind me.

Till now.

Last night, I dreamed the imp returned.
He inched his way out of the dim photo.
Plunked at my feet, eyebrows raised,
and saw that I no longer wore footie pajamas.
Then rubbed his eyes at the sight of my gray hair.

"As it is," Poe said.

"You will easily perceive that I am one
of the many uncounted victims of
the Imp of the Perverse."

"Ah," I say to the imp. "As it is.
And always has been."

It was he who lit the match,
that burned my cheeks with shame.
He who squeezed and squeezed
Until my lungs clenched.
"Does it pain you to know I haven't leapt
from the brink of the precipice?" I ask him.
Nor tossed my babies in a raging river?"

He doesn't reply, just straightens
his painted-on bow tie
and climbs upon my back.
Where he remains.
Glowing when he sparks my demented thoughts.
Edging screams to my throat during dusty sermons.
Urging the accelerator as I near a red light.

Silly little man from the garden of dismal flowers.
I paint his grin on my own lips.

Close my eyes and feel the dizzying expanse.
Knowing that he yawns and scratches.

Waiting, always, for me to jump.

The Gravedigger's Son

In the dead of winter, the grave digger's son prayed no one
would die. It wasn't a matter of wishing the town folk would live
forever. It was a matter of hoping they'd wait till spring thaw
to die. He winced when he remembered clearing snow from
gravesites and busting through frozen soil, one shovelful of
hard-earned dirt at a time. He said his father forbade backhoes
in the cemetery because machines tore up grass and headstones.
His father trusted only in strong backs pushing shovels deep
into the earth.

He told me this one afternoon as he leaned on his broom,
his eyes flashing a smile, his lips still grim. Relieved his grave-
digging days were long gone. He watched the contour of dust
settle on the windows of Hammond Hall. Noticed the tired eyes
of faculty. Teased about ball games and imaginary beer cans he
might find in our offices. Talked of retiring in the spring.

Dust swirls in the corners of Hammond Hall. His broom no
longer teases it away. We must survive the winter without his
prayers. A backhoe made easy work of December dirt. So it was,
they buried the gravedigger's son.

Shopping the Memorial Garden

It's Friday afternoon. If I were 30 years younger, I'd be ordering
two-fers at a dive bar. Instead, I'm walking the serene buffalo
grass of Memorial Gardens, looking for just the right piece of
real estate.

We're splitting a plot, my husband and me. Once your body's
just ashes, you can get two-fers on plots. It's really one hell of
a deal. I'm thinking of a night several years back. It was midnight
and I had come out to this very spot with three ghost hunters.
Their electromagnetic detector went haywire over by trees.
Then they swore the temperatures dropped from 50 to 45
because a spirit was sucking the heat out of the air. I thought it
was just getting cooler because it was night. What did I know
of ghosts?

No ghosts today. The sweltering sun would drive them back
underground.

There are some nice folks out here: my favorite piano professor;
the happy-go-lucky guy that cooked Maundy Thursday dinners
at church; the mailroom worker who never quite recovered
from the big newspaper layoff. Funny how I had forgotten
they all were dead.

On the north side is an unopened Miller Lite on some guy's monument. I'm glad it's not a grapefruit IPA or a crisp chardonnay. The temptation for me to defile it would be too great.

Looking west, there's a gently rolling field. It's a view I could get used to. But there's an oil pumping unit smack dab in the middle, dragging out dinosaur remains for truck fuel. A cruel reminder that we'll all be fossils one day.

We settle on C215. The vibe there is just right. A plot cozied up by shrubbery, but not so close that the roots might tickle us. It has an excellent view and is close enough to the road for a loved one to easily find, but far enough away to avoid accidental drive-overs.

I ask if we should bring a tent tonight. Camp out here, just to make sure it fits. My husband laughs, and I remember, we're not really the camping out sort.

Dear Beauty

I saw your ghost in the dingy sky.
Dreamed of your long dead crimson blooms.
Wind presses, depresses, undresses.
While winter's dirge plays on.
Fire ignites tall grasses, scorches the land to black.

Beauty, are you here beneath the ashes
or above the red-tinged sky?
Is it you in the shadow of the sycamore
where naked limbs carve out your name?
Urging me simply to wait.
Wait 'til blossoms peek from the gray
Wait 'til green blankets cling to the hills
Wait 'til you crawl inside my hollowness
Beg my eyes open to see you reborn.

This is **Dawne Leiker's** first published book of poetry. She has written for newspapers and for academia and is currently working on a messy fantasy novel. She has lived most of her life in western Kansas, not so far away from her great-grandparents' homesteads.